Buses, Coaches, Trolleyb
Recollections 1963-
Henry Conn
HORSFORTH
VIA WHITE CROSS
NO
THROUGH
ROAD
KYY508

First published in 2019

British Library Cataloguing in Publication Data

A catalogue record for this book is available from the British Library.

ISBN 978 1 85794 537 9

Silver Link Publishing Ltd
The Trundle
Ringstead Road
Great Addington
Kettering
Northants NN14 4BW

Tel/Fax: 01536 330588
email: sales@nostalgiacollection.com
Website: www.nostalgiacollection.com

Printed and bound in the Czech Republic

Title page **LEEDS** This wonderful view of Samuel Ledgard's KYY 508 was taken on 30 August 1965. This bus had entered service with Ledgard in April of that year, and when the company was purchased by West Yorkshire it was exported to the USA.

Contents

Photo	DESTINATIONS
1	**LEEDS** (Title page)
	1963
2	**LEICESTER**
3	**SHEFFIELD**
4	**SHEFFIELD**
5	**NOTTINGHAM**
	1964
6	**SCARBOROUGH**
7	**LEEDS**
8	**KEIGHLEY**
9	**SCARBOROUGH**
10	**LEEDS**

Acknowledgements

A number of the illustrations in this book are from the camera of Bob Gell. Without these views and the detailed notes on each, this book would not have been possible. My most sincere thanks to Bob – outstanding.

The PSV Circle Fleet Histories for the operators in this book and a number of issues of *Buses Illustrated* were also vital sources of information.

Photo	DESTINATIONS
11	**NOTTINGHAM**
12	**MORECAMBE**
13	**LEEDS**
14	**NOTTINGHAM**
	1965
15	**NOTTINGHAM**
16	**MANCHESTER**
17	**MANCHESTER**
18	**LONDON**
19	**NOTTINGHAM**
20	**NOTTINGHAM**
21	**NOTTINGHAM**
22	**LEEDS**
23	**NEWCASTLE-UPON-TYNE**
24	**STRATFORD-UPON-AVON**
25	**LEEDS**
26	**BRADFORD**

Introduction

If the Fifties were in black and white, the Sixties were in Technicolor. The 'Swinging Sixties' remain the defining decade for Britain.

One of the biggest, defining aspects of the 1960s was music. Although rock and roll began to have an effect on Britain in the 1950s, it wasn't until the early Sixties and the emergence of 'British Invasion' groups like the Beatles that music truly began its revolutionary changes. The Beatles are an excellent example of how music influenced the lives of young Britons. Although they continued the rock and roll genre of the 1950s for the early part of the decade, by 1967 *Sergeant Pepper's Lonely Hearts Club Band* had become the turning point in music and inspired other musicians, such as the Beach Boys and the Rolling Stones, to experiment with new sounds and develop innovative music. Their later albums included lyrics encouraging rebellion against authority, as seen in *Revolution*. Young people began to stand up for their beliefs and their individuality.

Recreational drugs were also synonymous with the Sixties and became more commonly used in the latter part of the decade. Images of the Woodstock festival show people high on marijuana and LSD, dancing in fields with paint on their faces and their hair flowing free. It was very difficult for anyone in show business to avoid becoming involved in drugs in some way and, as easily influenced young people looking for fun, many were encouraged to follow their idols and take hallucinogenic drugs. LSD made people feel happy and optimistic and helped bring about the 'hippie' movement. The effects of these drugs were also reflected in psychedelic art and films, bringing new, vibrant and exciting colours and patterns to the

1963

LEICESTER In St Margaret's bus station on 22 March is Midland Red No 4913 (913 KHA), which entered service from Coalville garage in March 1961 and remained there until August 1970, when it was transferred to Oldbury; it was sold for scrap from there in May 1973. *Bob Gell*

On this day the Beatles released their first album, Please Please Me, *in the United Kingdom.*

forefront. The film *Yellow Submarine*, with its combination of psychedelic pictures and music illustrates this perfectly.

Although the UK wasn't directly involved in the Vietnam War, British musicians such as John Lennon brought it to the attentions of British people through protests against the conflict. Songs like *Give Peace a Chance* showed people the horrors and pointlessness of war, and fans followed in the footsteps of their idols to pursue peace and freedom. This became one of the biggest aspects associated with the 'hippie' movement, when people began to challenge and question authority, something that would have been unheard of a decade earlier.

The Profumo Affair, a scandalous mix of sex, spies and government, captured the public's attention in 1963. Secretary for War John Profumo was discovered to have had an affair with a woman who was also seeing a Russian military attaché. Profumo denied the affair but later admitted that he had lied to the House of Commons and resigned. The affair changed the relationship between government and press for ever and seriously undermined the public's trust in politicians. The traditional deference to figures of authority was now gradually being replaced by suspicion and mistrust.

Fashion in the decade mirrored many of the social changes of the Sixties. Mary Quant became famous for popularising the mini-skirt, which became the epitome of 1960s fashion.

Feminism started to become a more influential ideology as more jobs became available to women in the Sixties. This allowed them to move away from home and become more independent. The contraceptive pill was

SHEFFIELD At Pond Street on 8 August 1963 is Sheffield Corporation A fleet No 900 (9000 WB), a Roe Dalesman-bodied AEC Reliance new in 1958. This was a one-off purchase for Sheffield, and was initially used for visits and inspections by the Transport Committee, but later used in service; it was noted working the 48 to Manchester via Woodhead on a number of occasions. Having a centre entrance made No 900 unsuitable for one-person operation, but it remained in the Sheffield fleet until 1970. *Bob Gell*

This day went down in history as the day of the 'Great Train Robbery' in Buckinghamshire.

legalised for all women in 1967 and gave them the opportunity to broaden their hopes and dreams far beyond motherhood and marriage. The Women's Liberation movement was in its infancy in 1968 when 850 women at the Ford factory in Dagenham went on strike, arguing for equal pay with their male co-workers. This action resulted in the passing of the Equal Pay Act of 1970. Furthermore, women were becoming increasingly involved in politics. For example, in 1968 Barbara Castle became the first and only woman to be appointed First Secretary of State, and women began to find a voice in society and the running of the country.

Technological advancements of the 1960s drastically changed how people spent their leisure time. Increases in employment and disposable income allowed people to spend more on leisure activities, and colour television and pocket transistor radios enhanced and broadened their free time. Most teenagers owned a transistor radio, allowing them to listen to pop music on the move. The microwave oven shortened the amount of time women spent in the kitchen, allowing them more freedom and time to enjoy themselves. By the end of the decade Neil Armstrong and Buzz Aldrin had achieved the impossible by becoming the first men on the Moon in 1969.

The 1960s was a decade of rapid change – blink for one second and you missed it. It was the period that finally allowed people the liberty and individuality they had fought for, something that we take for granted nowadays. The Sixties began bleak and restricted, but by the end people were full of hope and optimism for a better future.

Enjoy the Technicolor nostalgia...

SHEFFIELD Leaving for Bradford on the same day is Yorkshire Woollen No 895 (GHD 767), an MCCW-bodied Leyland PD3A/1 new in 1962. The all-red livery did very little for the spartan lines of the MCCW bodywork – a cream band would be added later above the lower-deck windows, which improved the looks a little. *Bob Gell*

20 biggest chart hits of 1963-69

Weeks at No 1	Year	Song and artist
8	1969	*Sugar Sugar*, Archies
7	1963	*From Me To You*, Beatles
	1966	*Green Green Grass of Home*, Tom Jones
	1967	*Hello, Goodbye*, Beatles
6	1963	*She Loves You*, Beatles
	1967	*Release Me (And Let Me Love Again)*, Engelbert Humperdinck
	1967	*A Whiter Shade of Pale*, Procul Harum
	1968	*Those Were The Days*, Mary Hopkin
	1969	*Get Back*, Beatles
	1969	*Two Little Boys*, Rolf Harris
5	1963	*I Want to Hold Your Hand*, Beatles
	1964	*I Feel Fine*, Beatles
	1965	*Tears*, Ken Dodd
	1965	*Day Tripper/We Can Work It Out*, Beatles
	1966	*Distant Drums*, Jim Reeves
	1969	*Honky Tonk Women*, Rolling Stones
4	1963	*I Like It*, Gerry and the Pacemakers
	1963	*You'll Never Walk Alone*, Gerry and the Pacemakers
	1964	*You're My World*, Cilla Black
	1966	*These Boots Are Made For Walkin'*, Nancy Sinatra
	1966	*The Sun Ain't Gonna Shine Anymore*, Walker Brothers
	1966	*Yellow Submarine/Eleanor Rigby*, Beatles
	1967	*I'm a Believer*, Monkees
	1967	*San Francisco (Be Sure to Wear Some Flowers in Your Hair)*, Scott McKenzie
	1967	*The Last Waltz*, Engelbert Humperdinck
	1967	*Massachusetts*, Bee Gees
	1968	*What a Wonderful World/ Cabaret*, Louis Armstrong
	1968	*Young Girl*, Gary Puckett and the Union Gap
	1968	*The Good, the Bad and the Ugly*, Hugo Montenegro and his Orchestra
	1969	*Where Do You Go To My Lovely*, Peter Sarstedt

NOTTINGHAM This is Eland Street in Basford on 10 October, where 8-foot-wide Brush-bodied BUT 9641Ts like No 514 (KTV 514) never normally ventured, but it is on a enthusiasts' tour of the trolleybus system. *Bob Gell*

On this day the second James Bond film, From Russia With Love, *opened in the UK.*

1964

SCARBOROUGH Leaving for Helmsley on 12 June is United No BU 508 (508 FHN), an ECW-bodied Bristol MW5G new in 1958.

On this day Nelson Mandela and seven co-defendants were sentenced to life imprisonment; Mandela would not be released until 1990.

Academy Awards, 1963-69

Year	Best Picture	Best Actor	Best Actress
1963	*Tom Jones*	Sidney Poitier (*Lilies of the Field*)	Patricia Neal (*Hud*)
1964	*My Fair Lady*	Rex Harrison (*My Fair Lady*)	Julie Andrews (*Mary Poppins*)
1965	*The Sound of Music*	Lee Marvin (*Cat Ballou*)	Julie Christie (*Darling*)
1966	*A Man for all Seasons*	Paul Schofield (*A Man for all Seasons*)	Elizabeth Taylor (*Who's Afraid of Virginia Woolf?*)
1967	*In the Heat of the Night*	Rod Steiger (*In the Heat of the Night*)	Katharine Hepburn (*Guess Who's Coming to Dinner*)
1968	*Oliver!*	Cliff Robertson (*Charly*)	Katharine Hepburn (*The Lion in Winter*)/Barbra Streisand (*Funny Girl*)
1969	*Midnight Cowboy*	John Wayne (*True Grit*)	Maggie Smith (*The Prime of Miss Jean Brodie*)

Below: **LEEDS** The bus depot in the background is Headingley on Otley Road, which was purchased from the Cardigan Estate in 1873 and extensively rebuilt in 1935. It was converted to bus operation after the closure of the Lawnswood tram route in 1956. Just passing the depot working route 33 is West Yorkshire No SG 139 (JWT 288), an ECW-bodied Bristol L5G new in 1950. The date is 19 June, and No SG 139 was withdrawn from service six months later.

On this day Boris Johnson was born in New York.

Above: **KEIGHLEY** Working local Keighley services on 22 June is Keighley-West Yorkshire No KDB 30 (GWX 125), an ECW-bodied Bristol K6B new in 1949; also in view is similar No KDB 34 (GWX 129). No KDB 30 would be withdrawn in September 1969 and pass into preservation, but No KDB 34 would not be so lucky and was scrapped in March 1967.

On this day in Exeter, New Hampshire, USA, Dan Brown, author of The Da Vinci Code, *was born.*

Below: **SCARBOROUGH** In the bus station on 3 July is United No BG 392 (LHN 834), an ECW-bodied Bristol L5G new in 1949; it would be withdrawn and sold to a dealer in December 1964, and was later noted as a site canteen in Bradford.

On this day the first organised protest against the Vietnam War was held outside the White House.

Above: **LEEDS** Leaving for Keighley on 6 July is West Yorkshire No DB 62 (JWY 230), an ECW lowheight-bodied Bristol KS6B that had been new in 1950 and was sold for scrap in February 1967.

The Beatles' first feature film, A Hard Day's Night, *premiered in London to 1,200 lucky ticket-holders at the London Pavilion.*

Above: **NOTTINGHAM** This view was taken on 12 July, and heading for Bulwell Market is Nottingham trolleybus No 570 (KTV 570), a Brush-bodied BUT 9641T new in February 1952; it would be sold for scrap in July 1965. No 801 (DAU 454) alongside is a Cravens-bodied AEC Regal that had been new to Nottingham in November 1937. In September 1959 it was withdrawn from service and became a mobile canteen, remaining in this role until sold for scrap in August 1968. *Bob Gell*

Above right: **MORECAMBE** On the seafront on 20 August is Morecambe & Heysham Corporation No 15 (GTJ 696), a Park Royal-bodied AEC Regent II new in May 1947. Also seen in this view is a good selection of popular early-1960s cars including a Morris Minor, Ford Anglia, Vauxhall Viva and Hillman Imp. No 15 was sold for scrap in 1966.

Right: **LEEDS** Service 54 was long the domain of the all-Leyland PD2/1s from 1950, so this view taken on 2 August of No 621 (NUB 621), a Roe-bodied AEC Regent III new in 1950, is quite rare. The 1950 Leylands would all be gone by November 1968, and No 621 would follow a year later.

The wreckage of a plane piloted by popular singer Jim Reeves was found near Brentwood, Tennessee, 42 hours after it crashed. Reeves's body had been thrown from the aircraft, while that of his manager, Dean Manuel, was found inside the plane.

Above: **NOTTINGHAM** For the whole of the 1950s Barton undertook a programme to produce new buses from old chassis. The bodywork was newly constructed in Barton's own workshops and was to a full-front design (a few chassis were bodied by outside contractors). The first 26 examples used pre-war chassis that had been largely acquired with their original bodywork, which was scrapped. No 635 (MAL 390) was built from two TD3 chassis acquired from Burnley and entered service in April 1951 with bodywork by Strachan. This view was taken on 12 August at Barton's depot at Chilwell; No 635 was withdrawn and sold for scrap in November 1965. *Bob Gell*

Above: **NOTTINGHAM** For the hundreds of Geordies who found work and settled in Coventry and Warwickshire in the uncertain days of the 1930s, the long-distance coach service run by Hall Brothers of South Shields was a lifeline to friends and relatives back home. On 12 August en route to Coventry is Hall Brothers' HCU 963, a Plaxton-bodied Leyland PSU3/3r new to Halls in June 1963 and sold in June 1967, a month before the company was purchased by Barton. *Bob Gell*

On this day the writer Ian Fleming, best known for his James Bond novels, died.

Left: **MANCHESTER** At Piccadilly on 28 September is brand-new Stockport No 21 (BJA 921B), an East Lancashire-bodied Leyland PD2/40. *Bob Gell*

On this day Harpo Marx, the one member of the Marx Brothers who did not speak during his film performances, died in Los Angeles.

Left: **MANCHESTER** At the same location on the same day is Manchester Corporation No 4048 (GVR 350), a Brush-bodied Daimler CVG5 new in 1950; it would be sold for scrap in 1968. In contrast, behind it is an Alexander-bodied Daimler CRG6LX in the fleet of North Western Road Car. *Bob Gell*

Right: **LONDON** Between January and September 1964 United Counties took delivery of ten ECW-bodied Bristol RELH6Gs, and representing this batch is No 253 (ABD 253G), standing in a corner of Victoria bus station on 29 September. All ten had air suspension, Gardner 6HLX engines, five-speed manual gearboxes and express-style coach seats; they were originally painted in all-over green with a cream waistband, but were soon modified as seen in this view with cream window surrounds. *Bob Gell*

NOTTINGHAM At Mount Street bus station in Nottingham on 9 April is Midland General No 507 (447 SNU), an ECW-bodied Bristol FSF6G new in 1962. *Bob Gell*

The Beatles' song Ticket to Ride *was released as a single on this day in the United Kingdom, and reached No 1 in the best-selling singles chart published five days later.*

NOTTINGHAM At Broad Marsh bus station on the same day is brand-new West Bridgford Urban District Council No 41 (BRR 241C), an East Lancashire-bodied AEC Renown. All the West Bridgford UDC buses would pass to Nottingham on 29 September 1969, and No 41, numbered 393 in the Nottingham fleet, would be one of the last West Bridgford buses to be withdrawn from service, in April 1976, and would be acquired by Castle Point Bus Company, Benfleet, for further service until November 1980, when it was sold for scrap. *Bob Gell*

NOTTINGHAM This view of Nottingham No 93 (93 RTO), an NCME-bodied Daimler CRG6LX, was taken on 23 February at Bulwell Market; the bus would be sold in January 1969. *Bob Gell*

Sadly on this day we lost the great Stan Laurel, half of the duo Laurel and Hardy.

LEEDS At the Otley depot of Samuel Ledgard on 30 April is LAE 12, an ECW-bodied Leyland PD1A that had been new to Bristol Omnibus in March 1948. In October 1960 Ledgard acquired it and placed it into service in February the following year. During April 1965 the seats were removed and the vehicle was used for towing at the Otley depot until the sale of the business on 14 October 1967.

NEWCASTLE-UPON-TYNE Between April and September 1957 Newcastle Corporation took delivery of its last half-cab buses, 20 Park Royal-bodied AEC Regent Vs and 10 Weymann-bodied Leyland PD3/1s. Representing the former group in the city centre on 2 June is No 174 (174 AVK), which would be sold for scrap in March 1970.

The Australian cricketing brothers Steve and Mark Waugh were born on this day in Canterbury, New South Wales.

New to TV, 1963-69

1963
Ready, Steady, Go!
Doctor Who

1964
Top of the Pops
Playschool
BBC2
Horizon

1965
Not Only … But Also
Public Eye
Thunderbirds
Jackanory

1966
Adam Adamant Lives!
Till Death Us Do Part

1967
At Last the 1948 Show
Callan
Do Not Adjust Your Set
The Forsyte Saga
The Prisoner

1968
Dad's Army
Magpie

1969
Monty Python's Flying Circus
Department S
Randall and Hopkirk (Deceased)
Mary, Mungo and Midge

NEWCASTLE-UPON-TYNE Passing under the trolleybus wires in the city centre on the same day is No 333 (NVK 333), an NCB-bodied AEC Regent III new in September 1950. Interestingly, after withdrawal from passenger service this bus was fitted for use as a snowplough in April 1969 but was sold for scrap four months later, I would suspect without having ploughed any snow.

STRATFORD-UPON-AVON At the Red Lion bus station on 12 June is Stratford Blue No 2 (669 HNX), a Willowbrook-bodied Leyland PD3A/1 new in 1963. Note that three of the buses in view have the silver roof livery, whereas on the left No 24 (MAC 571), an all-Leyland PD2/12 new to Stratford Blue in 1952, carries the repainted white roof. Stratford Blue passed to Midland Red on 1 January 1971 and, renumbered 2002 by Midland Red, No 2 remained in that fleet until December 1971. Acquired by Isle of Man Road Services in January 1972 and registered MN 45, it lasted in that fleet for just over ten years.

Above: **LEEDS** Leaving Wellington Street coach station on 23 June is West Yorkshire No EUG 81 (7902 WY), an ECW dual-purpose-bodied Bristol MW5G new in 1961. Nos EUG 81 to 89 were delivered in cream and red livery, the only EUGs to be delivered in those colours; they were also the first to be fitted with fluorescent lighting.

Right: **BRADFORD** Between February and June 1958 Bradford acquired a fleet of 25 AEC Regent IIIs from London Transport. One of the first to arrive was No 424 (HLX 243), a Park Royal-bodied example that had been new in October 1947. This view was taken on 3 July, and No 424 would be sold for scrap in September 1968. *Bob Gell*

The Football Association, the governing body of professional soccer in England, changed its rules on 3 July 1965 to allow teams to substitute players during a game. Previously, when a player was injured, no replacement was allowed. Initially a team could make only one substitution during the duration of the game.

EDINBURGH Carrying a hefty load of tourists, standing outside Holyrood Palace on 8 July is Edinburgh Corporation No 204 (204 SC), a Duple-bodied Bedford SB5 new in May 1963. After a short service career, No 204 was acquired by Moordale Bus Service in August 1971, eventually making its way to Mauritius by August 1977.

Little did these tourists know that Ronald Biggs would escape from Wandsworth Prison that afternoon and remain at large for almost 46 years.

ABERYSTWYTH On 13 July we see Western Welsh No 1104 (JBO 104), a Weymann-bodied Leyland PSUC1/1 new in October 1954. After withdrawal No 1104 passed to Morris of Pencoed, then to Llynfi Motors, entering service with that company in January 1970, and finally to Morriston Coaches in July 1976, where it was unfortunately destroyed by fire in October 1977.

Photo	DESTINATIONS
27	EDINBURGH
28	ABERYSTWYTH
29	BRISTOL
30	LEEDS
31	LAKE DISTRICT
32	LEEDS
33	SALFORD
34	LEICESTER
35	STOCKPORT
36	ASHTON-UNDER -LYNE
37	WALSALL
38	WEYMOUTH
39	LITTLEHAMPTON
40	LITTLEHAMPTON
	1966
42	MAIDSTONE
43	MAIDSTONE
44	LEEDS
45	BATH
46	LEEDS
47	LEEDS
48	LLANDOVERY
49	NEWQUAY
50	EDINBURGH
51	LEEDS
52	LEEDS

BRISTOL In Lawrence Hill depot on 1 August is No LC8444 (YHT 937), an ECW-bodied Bristol LD6B new in October 1957. It was sold to Top Deck Travel in September 1975 and was still owned by that company in December 1983. *Bob Gell*

On this day Jim Clark clinched the Formula 1 World Championship by winning the German Grand Prix.

LEEDS There were two slightly different hourly routes operated by Samuel Ledgard between Otley and Horsforth. One of them included a low stone-arched railway bridge over Henshaw Lane in Yeadon, which carried a short former Midland Railway branch line from Guiseley to Yeadon; used for freight traffic only, passenger trains having been withdrawn in 1954, the line closed completely in 1964. This view of KYY 502 was taken on 5 August; it is a Weymann lowheight AEC Regent III that had been new to London Transport in May 1950 and was acquired on 3 February 1965, entering service on 1 June. The bridge has since been demolished, but the abutments still remained in 2007.

LAKE DISTRICT In the beautiful Cumbrian hills and heading for Orton on 15 August is Ribble No 452 (FCK 884), a SARO-bodied Leyland PSUC1/1 new in early 1954. It would later pass to Locke & Sons of West Auckland, and by November 1979 had been acquired for preservation by the Ribble Vehicle Preservation Group.

On this day at the Shea Stadium in New York, the Beatles performed the first stadium concert in the history of rock, attended by 55,600 fans.

LEEDS In the background of this view taken on 30 August are the premises of Ford distributor Hayes of Horsforth, New Road Side; the building had been used as a fire station during the war. In 1965 you could buy from Hayes a new Cortina saloon for £573 6s 3d, including tax, a Corsair saloon for £653 1s 2d, a Capri coupé for £785 19s 7d, a Zephyr 6 for £836 14s, and a Zodiac saloon for £982 18s. The bus is Samuel Ledgard's KYY 502 again (see page 21).

SALFORD Between 1950 and 1952 Salford City Transport placed into service 195 Metro-Cammell-bodied Daimler CVG6s and a further 15 with Burlingham bodywork. Representing the 1952 Metro-Cammell-bodied batch is No 513 (FRJ 513). All the Daimlers featured straight staircases and traditional polished wood interior window frames, and for around ten years they were the backbone of the Salford fleet; apart from rush-hour traffic they were the only buses to be seen. This view was taken on 28 August 1965.

Singer Shania Twain was born on this day.

LEICESTER The business of Kemp & Shaw passed to Midland Red on 30 July 1955, although the company operated as a subsidiary until 1 January 1959. One of the buses that passed to Midland Red was No 4845 (JBC 989), an all-Leyland PD2/12 new to Kemp & Shaw in July 1950 and seen here on 9 September 1965. It remained in the Midland Red fleet operating from Leicester's Sandacre Street depot until withdrawal in May 1967. *Bob Gell*

On this day the Rolling Stones were at No 1 with their single (I Can't Get No) Satisfaction.

STOCKPORT The last Crossley bodies to be built were supplied to Stockport and fitted to Leyland PD2/30 chassis in August 1958; they were Stockport's first new double-deck buses since 1951. Of the batch of ten, numbered 337 to 342 and 333 to 336 (NDB 360 to 369), the last six were collected in a partly completed condition and finished by Stockport at its works, which sent former Crossley staff to the Crossley works to collect the missing parts. This view of No 340 (NBD 363) was taken on 10 September at Mersey Square in Stockport. *Bob Gell*

Above left: **ASHTON-UNDER-LYNE** Corporation was a Leyland user and had only the one batch of Guy Arab IVs with rare Bond bodywork, delivered in 1956. The usual home for the Guys was the route between Ashton and Mossley, and representing them is No 65 (XTC 852), seen in Ashton on 10 September. *Bob Gell*

Above: **WALSALL** Corporation acquired eight Park Royal -bodied Sunbeam F4 trolleybuses from Ipswich. The one seen here, Walsall No 351 (ADX 189), had been new to Ipswich in July 1950 is seen on 20 September 1965 at the terminus of the 29, a joint service between Wolverhampton and Walsall with termini at the Savoy Cinema in Walsall and St James Square in Wolverhampton. The 29 was discontinued on 31 October 1965 due to the building of the M6. No 351 passed to the West Midlands PTE on 1 October 1969 and was withdrawn and sold for scrap in May 1970.

The excellent Bad Moon Rising *by Creedence Clearwater Revival was the No 1 single on this day.*

Left: **WEYMOUTH** Between March and June 1957 East Kent took delivery of 12 Beadle-bodied AEC Reliances (MJG 41 to 52), and all were used for touring work until 1970. This is MJG 50, photographed on 29 September; all 12 had been withdrawn by 1976.

The No 1 single on this day was Tears *by the late Ken Dodd.*

Left: **LITTLEHAMPTON** Waiting for the conductor to board at the town's bus depot on 5 October is Southdown No 744 (LUF 244), an all-Leyland PD2/12 new in April 1952; it would be sold to Pearson, a contractor of Hetton-le-Hole, in August 1967.

The following day Ian Brady and Myra Hindley murdered their fifth and last victim; Brady was arrested on 7 October, and Hindley five days later.

Right: **LITTLEHAMPTON** On the same day we see No 759 (MUF 459), an NCME-bodied Leyland PD2/12 new in June 1953; it passed to Bexleyheath Transport in February 1968 and was sold for scrap in December 1969.

The Beatles' album Help! *would be replaced by* The Sound of Music *soundtrack as No 1 album on 10 October.*

1966

Below: **MAIDSTONE** No C427 (427 LKE) is a Harrington coach-bodied AEC Reliance new in September 1960, but by the time this view was taken, on 20 March, it had been downgraded to normal services. Interestingly, its destination is shown as Lenham Sanatorium, which had originally been designed to treat those suffering from TB; at the time it was built in 1914 the only known treatment was relaxation, good nursing and lots of fresh air. The first patients, however, were Canadian soldiers who had been gas-attacked in the trenches. By 1986 the hospital had been demolished for a new housing development.

Above: **MAIDSTONE** On layover in Maidstone on 5 March, the crew relax before their next duty in the lower deck of Maidstone & District No DH439 (RKP 920), a Weymann-bodied Leyland PD2/12 new in November 1953; it would be acquired by R. G. Turner of Darlaston in July 1967 and sold for scrap by March 1969.

On this day Nancy Sinatra was at No 1 with – you should be singing the song by now! – These Boots Are Made For Walkin'.

LEEDS This view of the junction of Boar Lane and Bishopgate Street, showing the old Yorkshire Banking Company building on the corner, was taken on 15 April. The bank was built in 1899 and was designed by W. W. Gwyther; two years after opening it was taken over by the London City & Midland Bank, later just the Midland. More recently, it has been occupied by the Observatory Wine Bar, then Flares nightclub. On service 24 to Halifax is Yorkshire Woollen No 805 (DHD 185), an MCCW-bodied AEC Regent V new in 1959; it passed to Hebble in 1970 but was sold for scrap without entering service in August of that year. The Leeds City bus on the right is No 376 (NNW 376), an all-Leyland PD2/1 new in 1950 and sold for scrap three months after this view was taken.

Above: **BATH** On 30 April the crew of Bath Services No 2967 (987 DAE), an ECW-bodied Bristol MW5G new in July 1959, are ready to depart from the city with a service to Weston. In September 1959 No 2967 was allocated to Bath Services, where it remained until March 1971 when it was transferred to the Bristol Omnibus depot at Trowbridge. By January 1972 it had returned to Bath, staying there until withdrawn in November 1974; acquired by Rivington Carpets, based in Highworth, in August 1976, it had been sold for scrap by December 1977.

On this day regular hovercraft services began between Ramsgate and Calais.

Below: **LEEDS** In Elland Road on 7 May, with Leeds United football ground in the background, is No 839 (WUA 839), a Roe-bodied AEC Regent V new in 1956. In the second picture the bus has turned and is ready for its return journey to the Corn Exchange.

On this day Leeds United were away to Burnley, winning 1-0. This was the last match of the 1965-66 season and Leeds United finished 6 points behind champions Liverpool.

LLANDOVERY is a small market town around 25 miles north-east of Carmarthen and 27 miles north of Swansea. About to leave for Haverfordwest on 14 May is Western Welsh No 1352 (DBO 352C), a Park Royal-bodied Leyland PSUC1/11 new in August 1965; it passed to South Wales Transport Company as part of the transfer of Haverfordwest services and depot in March 1972, and remained with that company until withdrawal in December 1976.

Manfred Mann's Pretty Flamingo *was the No 1 single on this day.*

NEWQUAY On 10 June we see Western National No 2074 (AUO 521B), an ECW-bodied Bristol FLF6G new in 1964. During May 1966, as seen here, No 2074 was repainted in the reversed livery of cream and green for use on the Newquay to St Ives express service.

On this day in San Francisco, Janis Joplin made her debut as a rock singer; very sadly she died at the tender age of 27 in October 1970.

EDINBURGH Heading west along Princes Street on 28 June is No 614 (YWS 614), an Alexander-bodied Leyland PD2A/30 new in January 1962; it would pass to Lothian Region Transport on 16 May 1975 and was sold for scrap in October 1976.

On this day one of my favourite actresses, Mary Stuart Masterson, was born in New York City.

LEEDS Leaving the West Yorkshire bus station on Templar Street for a local journey to Stanks on 9 July is West Yorkshire No SBW27 (KWU 387), an ECW-bodied Bristol LWL6B new in 1952. It was subsequently sold for scrap in January 1967.

On this day Jack Nicklaus won the British Open at Muirfield, Scotland.

LEEDS Empty and devoid of any movement at the bus station on the same day is West Yorkshire is No EUG 93 (MWY 619), an ECW-bodied Bristol LS6G new in 1954. To the right is No DX4 (MWY 113), a Bristol LD6G also bodied by ECW and new in 1954. No EUG 93 would be sold in October 1969 and No DX4 would follow a year later.

HALIFAX acquired ten Weymann-bodied Albion Nimbuses in 1963 to work on a few routes that, due to narrow roads and sharp bends, required a small bus. However, the Nimbus had a small 4.1-litre engine, was noisy and had difficulty climbing the Pennine hills. This is No 253 (RJX 253) working on service 61 on 30 July; it was later acquired by Baddeley Brothers of Holmfirth for use on that company's rural routes and lasted long enough to pass to West Yorkshire PTE in 1976 as a withdrawal.

On this day, 30 July 1966, England defeated West Germany in the World Cup final.

LITTLEHAMPTON This is Southdown No 6 (TCD 6) on 12 August. A Beadle Commer TS3 new in December 1956, it would be withdrawn in 1969 and was noted with Castrol Oils in Ellesmere Port by September 1970.

On this day three plain-clothes policemen were killed in Shepherds Bush, west London, in what later became known as the 'Massacre of Braybrook Street'.

Photo	DESTINATIONS
53	HALIFAX
54	LITTLEHAMPTON
55	HAYWARDS HEATH
56	MAIDSTONE
57	MAIDSTONE
58	PORTSMOUTH
59	GOSPORT
60	GOSPORT
61	LEEDS
62	CHESTERFIELD
63	NEWPORT
64	NEWPORT
65	WEYMOUTH
66	RAMSBOTTOM
67	BRADFORD
68	BRADFORD
69	EARLS COURT
70	MERTHYR TYDFIL
71	WEST BRIDGFORD
72	LEEDS
73	HONITON
74	CARDIFF
75	ABERYSTWYTH
76	BALA
77	BALA

HAYWARDS HEATH At the bus station on 15 August is Southdown No 517 (OUF 517), a Park Royal-bodied Guy Arab IV new in March 1955. It was sold to Davies of Tredegar in April 1968 and lasted just over a year in that operator's fleet before being sold for scrap.

The Beatles' Yellow Submarine/Eleanor Rigby *was the No 1 single on this day.*

MAIDSTONE Delivered to East Kent in February 1964 were 20 Park Royal-bodied AEC Regent Vs, and representative of this batch is AFN 774B at Maidstone bus station, indicating a journey to Folkestone on 17 August.

Above: **MAIDSTONE** On the same day in a quiet corner of Maidstone bus station is Maidstone & District No DH471 (VKO 995), a Weymann-bodied Guy Arab IV new in December 1955. This batch of Guy Arabs, Nos DH468 to 475, had been ordered by Chatham & District Traction Company, but the buses were not delivered until the company had been taken over. All were withdrawn in 1968.

Right: **PORTSMOUTH** Standing outside the Guildhall on 27 August is No 35 (EBK 572), one of a batch of 29 all-Crossley DD42/7Ts new in 1949. By 1965 the HOE7 engines and turbo-converters had been replaced by engines and gearboxes from withdrawn 1934 Leyland TD4s, and all 29 vehicles had been disposed of by 1967. *Bob Gell*

On this day Francis Chichester set off from Plymouth in his ketch Gypsy Moth IV *to sail around the world single-handed.*

Above: **GOSPORT** Seen on the same day, with the Ark Royal pub in High Street in the background, is Provincial No 16 (FCR 441), a Park Royal-bodied Guy Arab III new to Southampton Corporation in June 1948 and acquired by Provincial in February 1965; it would be sold for scrap in June 1970. *Bob Gell*

Above right: **GOSPORT** Gosport & Fareham's GOU 449 was an AEC Regal that used the chassis of Tilling GN 7271, which had been new in 1931. It was fitted with an AEC 7.7-litre diesel engine and a rear-entrance Reading body before entering service in 1949, then rebodied again, as seen here, also on 27 August, with a front-entrance Reading body in 1959. GOU 449 was withdrawn and sold for scrap in 1970. *Bob Gell*

Right: **LEEDS** A few buses await the fans from the Leeds United football game against Manchester United on 27 August. The Leeds team on this day included Bremner, Hateley, Hunter, Lorimer, Giles and Greenhoff, while the Manchester United team included Styles, Law, Best and Charlton. Leeds won 3-1, with goals from Lorimer, Reaney and Madeley; George Best scored for United. The bus is No 466 (MUG 466), a Roe-bodied AEC Regent III new in 1949 and sold for scrap in November 1968.

CHESTERFIELD Just delivered from the bodybuilders MCW, and still to receive its fleet number, this is East Midland's GNN 186D, one of the very last Albion Lowlander LR7s built in 1966. East Midland chose manual Lowlanders (having previously bought lowbridge Atlanteans) because the engine-braking available suited some of the company's hillier routes in the Peak District, notably routes 4 (Chesterfield-Doncaster) and 17 (Chesterfield-Matlock). The only modifications over a full service life of around 15 years were the removal of illuminated advertising displays from the first batch and the panelling over of the lower set of apertures in the radiator grille, as the engine was originally over-cooled in the upland climate in which these buses operated. *Bob Gell*

On this day, 29 August 1966, the Beatles played their final concert; thereafter only playing in the studio with the exception of their unscheduled rooftop concert on the Apple Records building on 30 January 1969.

NEWPORT On a private hire on 15 September is Western Welsh No 283 (WKG 283), a Willowbrook dual-purpose-bodied AEC Reliance new in August 1961. Originally delivered in the dual-purpose livery of wine red and ivory, No 283 was repainted in November 1964 in the then new blue and royal ivory dual-purpose livery, as seen here. It passed to South Wales in January 1972, and to Crosville three months later; it was sold for scrap by Crosville in November 1974.

NEWPORT In contrast to the previous view taken shortly afterwards on the same day, this is Western Welsh No 1272 (UKG 272), an MCCW dual-purpose-bodied Leyland PSUC1/2 new in January 1961, and carrying the wine red and ivory dual-purpose livery. No 272 was demoted to bus duties in May 1967 and was repainted in bus livery; it was sold to McAlpine in October 1973 for staff transport, lasting until January 1979.

On this day, 15 September 1966, the Royal Navy launched HMS Resolution *in Barrow-in-Furness, its first submarine capable of firing nuclear missiles.*

WEYMOUTH Between January and April 1958 Western Welsh took delivery of 18 Harrington-bodied AEC Reliances, Nos 101 to 118 (OUH 101 to 118), and this view of No 115 was taken on 25 September. The coach was sold to Office Cleaning Services of London in December 1967, and later operated with Beasley and Beale, both in Hounslow, before being sold for scrap in October 1973.

RAMSBOTTOM Photographed on 1 October, this is Ramsbottom Urban District Council No 3 (9459 TE), an East Lancashire-bodied Leyland PD2A/30 new in 1963. Ramsbottom UDC had one of the smallest bus fleets in the UK – in 1966 the operational fleet totalled 12 vehicles.

Above: **BRADFORD** In Chester Street bus station is Yorkshire Woollen No 587 (HD 7870). This bus started its service life in 1948 as a Brush-bodied Leyland PS1 and in 1955 was rebodied, as seen here on 9 October, with an MCCW 'Orion' H30/26 body. No 587 was sold to Georges Coaches of Kirkburton in April 1967 and sold for scrap in March 1968.

David Cameron, former British Prime Minister, was born in Marylebone, London, on this day.

Above right: **BRADFORD** Also in Chester Street bus station on that October day is Hebble No 280 (PCP 406), a Northern Counties-bodied AEC Regent 5 new in March 1962; withdrawn in February 1971, it would pass to Kitching of Goosenargh in June 1971, where it remained until August 1973. It was noted in September 1975 with Spook Sunday Markets Ltd, Moreton-in-Marsh.

Right: **EARLS COURT** At the Earls Court Motor Show on 19 October is Duple Commander Daimler SRC6 Demonstrator CWK 641C. *Bob Gell*

The day before this view was taken the Ford Cortina Mark II was launched.

MERTHYR TYDFIL Seen on 2 March is Red & White No L154 (MAX 130), an ECW-bodied Bristol LD6G new in 1954. Behind is Merthyr Tydfil No 109 (BHB 309), an East Lancashire-bodied Leyland PD3/4 new in 1960.

The No 1 single on this day was Engelbert Humperdinck's Release Me.

WEST BRIDGFORD
Acquired by West Bridgford UDC in April 1955 were two Duple-bodied Daimler CWA6s that had been new to Huddersfield in July 1945. Registered CCX 777 and CCX 779, they were given fleet numbers 24 and 27 in the West Bridgford fleet. This view of No 24 was taken on 18 March; it was subsequently withdrawn in October 1967 and passed into preservation. *Bob Gell*

On this the day the oil tanker Torrey Canyon *ran aground on Pollard's Rock between the Cornish mainland and the Isles of Scilly; ultimately 32 million gallons of oil were released, much of which washed up on the Cornish coast.*

Above: **HONITON** On private hire at Honiton on 23 April is Maidstone & District's No SC77 (HKT 577D), a Marshall dual-purpose-bodied AEC Reliance new in November 1966.`

On this day James Earl Ray escaped from Missouri State Penitentiary. On 4 April 1968 he would assassinate Dr Martin Luther King in Memphis and would remain at large until recaptured in London on 10 June.

Below: **LEEDS** This view taken on 5 May is looking north-west across Bridge Road towards Thrift Stores Ltd, a company that had many stores, mostly corner shops, in the city but, with the advent of larger supermarkets, shut down in the early 1970s. Working service 44 to Halton Moor is No 468 (MUG 468), a Roe-bodied AEC Regent III new in 1949 and sold for scrap in November 1968.

Photo	DESTINATIONS
78	LEEDS
79	LEEDS
80	WAKEFIELD
81	WAKEFIELD
82	LEEDS
83	LEEDS
84	LEEDS
85	LEEDS
	1968
86	LEEDS
87	WINCHESTER
88	WINCHESTER
89	LEEDS
90	LEEDS
91	CHELTENHAM
92	WINCHESTER
93	WINCHESTER
94	BEAULIEU

	1969
95	ASHFORD
96	WALSALL
97	ABERGAVENNY
98	ABERGAVENNY

Photo	DESTINATIONS
99	HYTHE
100	TODMORDEN
101	WEYMOUTH

CARDIFF In the bus station on 10 May is Western Welsh No 27 (WKG 27), a Weymann-bodied Albion NS3AN new in May 1961. It was fitted for one-person operation when delivered and had, as seen in this view, crests in place of the fleet name. In March 1968 it would donate its bodywork to a Bristol LHS6L and the chassis and engine would be dismantled for spares.

BALA This is Crosville No DFB 48 (261 SFM), an ECW-bodied Bristol FLF6B new in March 1961. Behind it in this 21 June view is No DLB 733 (VFM 598), an ECW-bodied Bristol LD6B new in July 1955.

The excellent single A Whiter Shade of Pale *by Procul Harum was the No 1 single on this day. (If you like Jimi Hendrix and have not yet discovered Robin Trower, who was with Procul Harum at this time, give him a listen on the album* Bridge of Sighs.*)*

ABERYSTWYTH Delivered to Western Welsh between July and August 1966 were ten Marshall dual-purpose-bodied Leyland PSUC1/12Ts, numbered 1375 to 1384 (HBO 375D to 384D). All ten were fitted with luggage lockers at the rear when new, and were delivered, as seen in this view of No 1378 on 20 June, in the blue and ivory dual-purpose livery. No 1378 passed to South Wales Transport in January 1972 and remained in that company's fleet until January 1977.

Above: **BALA** Also in Bala on the same day was No CUG 301 (OFM 673), an ECW coach-bodied Bristol LS6G new in 1952. This coach was fitted with a Gardner 6HLW 8.4-litre engine and had the earliest type of LS coach body with a single-piece windscreen and curved front corner windows; the livery was cream with black window surrounds. In 1960 No CUG 301 was fitted with jackknife doors and bus-type destination indicators, and during 1967 was fitted for one-person operation, passing to Jenkins of Skewen in January 1971.

Right: **LEEDS** Leaving for Otley on 16 July is Samuel Ledgard's ARN 394, a Leyland PD1 that had bodywork designed by Leyland but sub-contracted to Alexander. It was new in October 1946 to Preston Corporation, and was acquired by Ledgard in November 1961, entering service in January 1962 and remaining in the fleet until Ledgard was sold to West Yorkshire in October 1967. It was never operated by West Yorkshire and was sold for scrap in January 1968.

On this day the American comedian and actor Will Ferrell was born in California.

LEEDS Ledgard acquired four all-Leyland PD1As from Ribble via a dealer in September 1961; registered BCK 414, 415, 421 and 422, they entered service with their new operator in October/November 1961. This view of BCK 422 working the Otley to Leeds service was taken on 16 July; this bus would be sold for scrap six months later without operating for its new owner, West Yorkshire.

WAKEFIELD In the bus station on 18 July is West Riding No 695 (CHL 166), an all-Leyland PD2/1 new in 1950. At the stand behind, about to work a 57 to Bradford, is No 975 (WHL 975), a 1963 Roe-bodied Guy Wulfrunian. A number of the 1950 Leyland PD2/1s would have extended service lives because of the problems with the Wulfrunians; No 695 would be sold for scrap in June 1969 and No 975 would follow just ten months later after less than seven years in service.

Born on this day in New York was actor Mark Sinclair Vincent, better known to many as Vin Diesel.

WAKEFIELD Delivered new to West Riding in March 1956 were five Roe-bodied Guy Arab IVs, Nos 782 to 786 (HHL 994 to 998). In the bus station on 5 August is No 784 (HHL 996), which would be sold for scrap in March 1971.

On this day Pink Floyd released their first album, The Piper at the Gates of Dawn.

LEEDS In October 1966 Samuel Ledgard acquired from Tyneside GTY 169, a Metro-Cammell-bodied Leyland PD2/12 new in 1954. This view was taken on 13 August, and the bus has two months of further service with Ledgard before the sale to West Yorkshire; it would then be acquired by Carter's Coaches of Wendover, in whose fleet it remained until July 1970.

On this day the legendary rock band Fleetwood Mac made their debut at the National Jazz and Blues Festival in Windsor, Berkshire.

Below: **LEEDS** In service to Rawdon on the same August day is NCY 855, one of four Weymann-bodied AEC Regent Vs new in 1955/56 and purchased by Ledgard from South Wales Transport. This bus was new in July 1956, was acquired via a dealer in July 1967, and was put into service the same month. It was one of only 14 buses taken into stock by West Yorkshire out of Ledgard's fleet of 100-odd vehicles, on 14 October 1967. West Yorkshire sold NCY 855 in November 1969 and a month later it was purchased by Smith of Reading and entered service with that fleet in January 1970.

Above: **LEEDS** Kippax & District operated a service from Ledston Luck via Kippax, Garforth and Halton to Leeds. Later, a branch service was commenced during the day on weekdays via Ninelands Lane at Garforth instead of the normal A63 and Lidgett Lane. In service to Leeds on 15 October is 556 DUA, a Roe-bodied Leyland PD3A/1 new to Kippax in 1962. Wallace Arnold had purchased Kippax & District on 1 June 1956, but it continued to operate as a subsidiary until 31 March 1968, when Wallace Arnold sold it to Leeds Corporation. This bus was subsequently sold to Stonier's, with whom it remained operational until early 1978 when it was withdrawn, requiring too much work to pass the Certificate of Fitness.

LEEDS In Wellington Street on 3 December is newly repainted West Yorkshire No DGW12 (XUG 141), a Burlingham-bodied Daimler CVG6 that had been new to Samuel Ledgard in April 1957 and was one of the few buses that West Yorkshire retained for service after purchasing Ledgard in October 1967.

On this day Dr Christiaan Barnard and a team of surgeons and nurses performed the first heart transplant in Cape Town, South Africa.

LEEDS Farsley & Company's original route was operated between Stanningley and Rodley, via Farsley, on the outskirts of Leeds, and the company never expanded beyond this single service, although the route was later extended. This is MUB 433, a Daimler CVD6 that had been new to parent company Wallace Arnold in 1949 with Wilks & Meade C33F bodywork. The bus received a Plaxton FC35F body in 1954 before receiving the Roe bodywork seen in this view, taken a couple of days before Farsley's last day of operation. On 31 March 1968 Wallace Arnold sold the company to Leeds Corporation, and the last day of working by Farsley vehicles was Saturday 30th, when MUB 433 worked the last service journey from Pudsey to Rodley, returning at 23.15 to Stanningley only, thus ending nearly 50 years of the Farsley Omnibus Company.

WINCHESTER This is WCG 103, a Weymann-bodied Leyland PSUC1/1 new to King Alfred in 1959 and photographed in Winchester on 27 March 1968. On 29 April 1973 the business was acquired by Hants & Dorset, and this bus received fleet number 2703 and was quickly converted to one-person operation. In June 1973 it was repainted in National Bus Company livery, but was withdrawn the following year.

WINCHESTER Seen on the same day, this is WCG 107, a Park Royal-bodied AEC Bridgemaster new in 1959; when new it had an AEC AV590 9.6-litre engine with air suspension on the dropped centre rear axles, independent coil suspension on the front, and, as seen here, sliding cab doors.

On this day Yuri Gagarin, the first man to travel in outer space, was killed in an air crash.

LEEDS Indicated to go to Rothwell on 2 April is brand-new No 189 (MHL 189F), a Roe-bodied Daimler CRG6LX.

On this day Stanley Kubrick's 2001: A Space Odyssey *premiered in Washington DC.*

LEEDS Leaving every half-hour from the stand in King Street, Hebble service 28 took just under 2 hours to reach Rochdale. It was rare to see a double-deck bus on the 28 but, judging by the passenger load on Hebble's No 275 (GCP 5), a lowbridge Weymann-bodied AEC Regent V new in May 1956, two decks were required. This view was taken on 3 May 1968, and No 275 would be sold for scrap in June of the following year.

On this day the first heart transplant in the UK was performed by Dr Donald Ross and his team in London; the patient, Frederick West, would survive for 46 days before dying from complications arising from an infection.

CHELTENHAM Working a local service on 25 June is Cheltenham & District's No 8561 (UHY 374), an ECW-bodied Bristol KSW6G new in 1955. Out of service in 1975, No 8561 would pass to Classic Buses Limited, then to Cotswold Gliding Club in 2001 before being purchased for preservation in December 2015.

On this day Tony Hancock died in his flat in Bellevue Hill in Sydney, Australia, aged just 44.

WINCHESTER Just south of Winchester is a prominent Iron Age earthwork called Oliver's Battery; the name dates back to the English Civil War and is associated with Oliver Cromwell's siege of Winchester in 1645. About to leave for Oliver's Battery on 30 September is King Alfred's 323 CAA, a Park Royal-bodied AEC Bridgemaster new in 1961.

On this day at Everett, Washington, the Boeing 747, then the largest passenger plane ever built, was rolled out for the media and public to view.

WINCHESTER New in 1950, HOR 493 was an all-Leyland PD2/1 in the King Alfred fleet and is seen here in the city on the same day. It was withdrawn from service before King Alfred was sold to Hants & Dorset on 29 April 1973.

BEAULIEU It would appear from this view that one passenger is not too keen on looking at the wonderful old cars at the National Motor Museum at Beaulieu on 6 October! This is Ribble No 1042 (PCK 624), a Harrington-bodied Leyland L2T new in August 1961; it would be sold to Hills of Tredegar in October 1971, and by September 1976 was noted in the fleet of Potter of Skewen.

1969

ASHFORD At the East Kent depot on 6 January are NFN 337, a Beadle-bodied AEC Reliance new in 1957, and by comparison on the left KFN 232, a Weymann-bodied AEC Reliance new in 1955. NFN 337 would be sold in April 1971 and was noted on a farm in Northamptonshire in March 1975, while the Weymann-bodied AEC would be sold for scrap in September 1974.

On this day the 'Waverley' railway route between Edinburgh and Carlisle saw its last passenger services.

Above: **WALSALL** At the bus station on 20 May is Walsall's No 346 (ADX 915), a Park Royal-bodied Sunbeam F4 new to Ipswich in July 1959 and acquire by Walsall in February 1962. Another of the former Ipswich Sunbeam F4s, No 344 (ADX 193), waits behind. Both were sold for scrap in May 1970.

Another excellent single, Get Back *by the Beatles, was the No 1 single on this day.*

Below: **ABERGAVENNY** In the town's Red & White depot on 23 June is No U 362 (13 FAX), an ECW-bodied Bristol MW6G new in February 1963. Note the destination display 'Glascoed (R.O.F.)' – at its peak the Royal Ordnance Factory at Glascoed boasted nearly 700 separate buildings, each designated for a particular process and used as required. It still has in excess of 10 miles (16km) of roads, an 8-mile (13km) perimeter fence and, until more recent years, its own 17-mile (27km) standard-gauge railway system; the latter included a dedicated passenger station and freight marshalling yards, and was linked to the former Great Western Railway branch line between Pontypool Road and Monmouth. This rail link enabled the three-times-daily movement of up to 13,000 workers in and out of the site as well as the receipt of raw materials and components and the despatch of finished munitions. A small housing estate was built close by to accommodate managers and staff who had to respond quickly in emergencies.

ABERGAVENNY This is Red & White's No U 264 (DAX 602C), an ECW-bodied Bristol MW6G photographed on 1 July.

On this day Prince Charles was invested as Prince of Wales at Caernarfon; a couple of days later Brian Jones, founder member of the Rolling Stones, drowned in his swimming pool at his home in Sussex.

HYTHE Between March and June 1954 East Kent took delivery of 30 Duple Ambassador-bodied Dennis Lancet UFs, HJG 3 to 32. This is HJG 4 on 16 July; it would be withdrawn from service during the year and sold to a farm in Preston in August 1970.

On this day Apollo 11 lifted off towards the first landing on the Moon.

TODMORDEN Maidstone & District purchased 15 Harrington-bodied Albion Nimbus NS3ANs new in 1960, and representing them on 10 August is 307 LKK, still in Maidstone & District livery but now in the fleet of B&S Motors of Todmorden. Withdrawn a year later by B&S, the bus was acquired by Nelson Youth Centre, where it remained until sold for scrap in October 1973.

At this time in Los Angeles the members of the Manson family were invading the house of Roman Polanski and his wife Sharon Tate.

Index to locations and operators

WEYMOUTH Photographed on 17 September is Western Welsh's No 176 (OUH 176G), a Plaxton-bodied Leyland PSU3A/4RT new in April 1969. It had a five-speed semi-automatic gearbox, a two-speed rear axle and exhaust brakes from new.